(UN)DONE

ISBN: 979-8-9997641-2-6

This book is a work of non-fiction/poetry based on real-life experiences and personal emotions.

A wound that became part of me.

Design and illustration: Selena Santos

Some images in this book were created using artificial intelligence as an artistic tool, designed and edited under the author's vision and supervision.

Selena Santos

For you,

who, even with a heart shattered into a thousand pieces

and a soul held together by threads,

still keep trying.

Prologue

(UN)DONE. It walks that fine line between something falling apart and something completed — playing with what is broken and what is finished, with what once was and is no longer. Sometimes, language itself becomes part of the ache. Some things are easier said, others are felt in silence. This book speaks in the pauses, in the words that don't quite translate—because some pain lives beyond vocabulary.

This book doesn't promise healing or neatly closed chapters. It's not meant to impress. It's meant to be felt. It offers you a fogged-up mirror, where the reflection still trembles with what hurts — with what *still* hurts. Inside, you'll find half-truths, emotions that still bleed, memories that weigh heavy... but no longer crush.

This book doesn't try to give you answers, only to make you feel a little less alone while you search for them. Because sometimes, that's enough to keep going.

(UN)DONE isn't just a collection of poems; it's an emotional map. The timeline of a heart breaking without knowing if it's falling apart or rebuilding itself. You'll find pain here, yes. Nostalgia, too. But above all, you'll find truth — raw, imperfect truth, sometimes whispered, sometimes screamed — the kind that only dares to come out when no one's watching... or when you finally decide to look at yourself.

(UN)DONE

This book begins where most go silent: in the middle of the tremble. And it moves forward — slowly, but with soul — toward a kind of understanding that doesn't erase the past, but learns to hold it without letting it hurt the same.

Don't expect happy endings here. Expect something braver: someone who chose to move forward with their heart still in their hands.

Let it touch the parts you try to hide. Even if it hurts. Even if it stirs something in you. Even if it reminds you. Because sometimes, survival sounds quieter than we imagined — and healing doesn't always look like light, but rather like learning to live with the dark without letting it consume you.

This book didn't come to save you.

But maybe it will sit with you... right there, where it still hurts.

Poetry is a way of saying what we sometimes don't even understand ourselves—until we write it or read it.

It has the ability to express what the heart feels long before the mind can make sense of it. In poetry, I found comfort—a refuge.

When I didn't know how to cry, it cried for me. When I couldn't speak, it lent me words that said exactly what hurt. I hid between verses like someone hiding under the covers when the world feels too heavy.

And there, in the silence of a page, I felt less alone. Poetry didn't judge me. It didn't ask for explanations. It simply held me— as if it understood that, even in pieces, I was still worthy of love.

Some people call it poetry.

I call it — soul-thoughts —

small fragments of everything I never knew how to

say out loud;

because writing them became the way I learned to

BREATHE again.

Selena Santos

THE FALL

The Hero Who Wasn't

He promised to be my superhero.

The one who'd show up just in time,

the one who'd save me from the chaos,

the one who'd heal what others had broken.

He spoke of battles won,

of invisible shields,

strong arms where the world wouldn't hurt.

And I...

I believed him.

But the rescue never came.

The cape tore under lies.

And the arms that once promised peace

ended up pushing me deeper.

He promised to be my superhero,

but he became the villain:

the one who left new wounds,

the one who made me fear what I once longed for,

the one who fought...

but against me.

(UN)DONE

And now I understand that sometimes,

danger doesn't come with claws or shadows,

but with smiles and promises.

And that true heroes

don't make promises.

They stay.

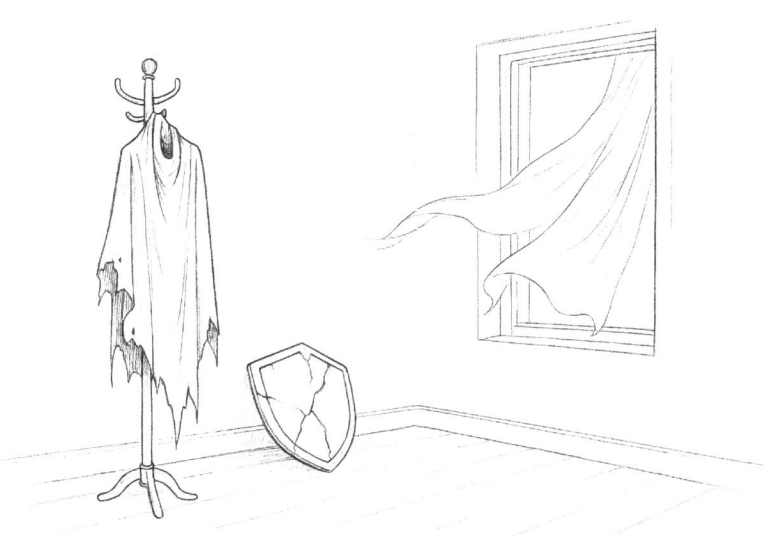

3:00 AM

Silence doesn't exist.

In its place,

the broken cries of a little girl

and the heavy snores of a woman who no longer

dreams.

Between them,

my mind—

a room with no doors,

filled with voices that won't quiet,

thoughts that push, that scream,

that won't let me breathe.

And me...

I could only think of one thing:

Why?

Why me?

Why this?

As if asking it

one more time

could change something.

As if someone—*anyone*—

might hear me.

What Did I Do?

I loved you

in quiet ways—

through soft words,

through waiting,

through every little thing

that said "I'm here."

But one day,

you stopped looking at me

like I was home.

You didn't yell.

You didn't break anything.

You just left.

And somehow,

that hurt more

than any goodbye.

I stayed,

replaying every second

like a broken film,

searching for the moment

(UN)DONE

I lost you without noticing.

What did I do?

Where did I go wrong?

when all I ever did

was love you

the best way I knew how.

I don't want to hate you.

I just want to understand.

Because I'm still awake at night,

waiting for an answer

you'll never give.

A Heaven No More

At first, your voice felt like home.

Your arms, like shelter.

Your silences, like rest.

I could lie against your chest and feel the world stop—

like nothing bad could touch me

as long as you were near.

And then...

everything changed.

Not all at once,

but like the sky falling in slow motion:

a colder word,

a look that cut,

an absence heavier than your presence.

I began walking in your footsteps

like someone walking barefoot on shattered glass—

afraid to speak,

afraid to stay quiet,

afraid of everything.

(UN)DONE

I grew smaller in your spaces.

Invisible.

Silent.

Until I no longer recognized myself.

And that's how I knew:

when I could no longer sleep peacefully with you near,

when my body stopped relaxing at your touch,

when your name

stopped sounding like peace...

That's when I understood the most heartbreaking

truth of all:

to fear the very one

who once

felt like refuge.

I Told You So

I don't know if *I'm* the problem,

but they taught me this way:

to smile even when it tore me apart,

to swallow my tears before anyone could see them,

to hide everything bad

just to avoid hearing

"I told you so."

I grew up learning that speaking up was exposing

myself,

that making mistakes meant shame,

that feeling too much made you weak,

and that trusting someone...

was handing them ammunition to use against you.

So I started keeping it all in—

the fears, the mistakes, the falls.

I perfected the art of pretending.

I got really good at saying *"I'm fine"*

when everything inside me was screaming for help.

Because when I showed the wound,

they didn't offer comfort—

they gave me guilt.

They reminded me I *"should've known better,"*

that *"they warned me,"*

that *"I brought it on myself."*

And then I learned something even crueler:

that it was safer to suffer in silence

than to fail out loud.

But sometimes I wonder…

How much of me got lost in that habit?

How many times did I need help and deny it to myself

just to avoid disappointing someone?

I don't know if *I'm* the problem. Maybe I am.

Or maybe I'm just the result of growing up in a world

where making mistakes

was worse than breaking on the inside.

(UN)DONE

No Way Out

I followed you,

thinking you were a way out.

An escape.

A way to run from the pain I was already carrying.

But you turned out to be just another entrance—

an entrance to a new wound,

another fall,

one more heartbreak.

You were so far from being a way out...

and I was so blind,

so desperate for relief,

that I ignored all the signs.

The red flags were waving,

but I only saw the wind.

Your distance was obvious,

but I mistook the silence for peace.

And yes...

It was my fault.

For not seeing what was clear.

(UN)DONE

For trusting without asking.

For waiting for you without conditions.

I just followed you.

No questions.

No defenses.

No sense of danger.

I followed—just like that.

And now it's up to me

to climb out of the place

where you were never the way out.

From the place

only I can rescue myself.

Here. Then Not.

I wanted you to see me.

I wanted you to want to see me.

But your words—

those that still echo without permission—

didn't embrace.

They cut.

I can't hate you,

but I can't love you either.

As if that were enough.

As if the silence that followed

didn't shatter me into a thousand pieces.

You weren't the storm... but you weren't the shelter

either.

You were that gray space

where love doesn't grow

and resentment never dies.

And I stayed there,

in the middle of your unspoken limits,

trying to understand how to love someone

who didn't know how to,

who couldn't,

or simply didn't want to

love me fully.

With You

You took my smile.

You took my dreams.

And you left me alone.

Alone... with the absence.

Absence of color,

absence of meaning,

absence of everything that once was mine.

Tell me—

What must I do for you to give the colors back?

For the world to stop looking so gray

since you left?

Roses

He gave me roses,

but never warned me they had thorns.

I took them with hope,

not knowing I would bleed from holding on.

They were beautiful—

as beautiful as his voice when he promised me the

sky,

as cruel as his silence afterward.

It wasn't the gift that hurt.

It was the way he gave it

without telling me

it would hurt too.

You Prove Me Right

I was afraid you'd hurt me.

But hurting me wasn't enough...

you destroyed me—

without mercy,

without pause,

without looking back.

It wasn't just the pain—

it was the way you caused it,

as if my heart

wasn't even worth

a single breath from you.

Too Late

It's so cruel

that you have to be dying

for others to finally realize

you needed help.

As if pain only matters

when it bleeds on the outside.

As if the scream within

doesn't count

unless it breaks glass.

They see you crawl,

but assume you're walking.

They see your silence,

and call it strength.

They see you smile,

never imagining

you're already saying goodbye

on the inside.

And then,

when the light fades,

when the body can't pretend anymore,

that's when they ask:

"Why didn't you say something?"

As if you hadn't been saying it

all along—

in silence.

A Miracle I Didn't Touch

I'll always carry the guilt.

For not holding you tighter,

for letting you go

when you were trembling the most.

I was a coward.

And I knew it the moment

your footsteps walked away

and I didn't run after them.

It wasn't that I didn't love you—

It was fear.

It stole my voice,

my hands,

my entire soul.

And now I think of you

like someone remembers a miracle

they didn't dare to touch,

afraid of breaking it.

You wanted me to fight,

and I gave you silence.

Selena Santos

You wanted fire,

and I was barely a spark.

Forgive me.

Not for losing you,

but for not trying to stop the loss.

For believing that love was enough,

without showing it.

This is what I'll carry forever:

not your absence,

but my surrender.

Because it was you...

and I was the one

who walked away.

— 02:18

Tell Me

And tell me,

how do I fill the emptiness you left behind?

Because I've tried everything.

I've spoken to strangers

who don't even know your name

but still hear my broken laughter

as if they could somehow mend it.

I've slept where I didn't belong.

searching for the warmth

you took from me,

and still—

I woke up cold.

I've filled my days with noise,

my nights with insomnia,

my soul with things I don't need

just to stop thinking of you.

But nothing works.

Nothing fits.

(UN)DONE

Because your absence

isn't just a hole—

it's an abyss.

So tell me...

how do you fill a void that was always yours.

I Forgot Where a Left Myself

This house

doesn't feel like home.

The walls look at me,

but they don't recognize me.

I don't feel like myself.

I inhabit my skin,

but I can't find my soul.

Where did I lose my way?

Which corner of myself did I vanish into, that I

no longer know the way back?

Something is broken,

something is missing—

a voice that used to be mine

and now only whispers.

And I don't know if it's sadness,

emptiness,

or just the echo

of everything I left behind

when I stopped feeling like me

Absence With a Voice

You didn't leave emptiness...

you left silence.

A silence that creaks at dawn,

that weighs more than any broken word.

You didn't take the colors...

you took the light.

And even though the world keeps turning,

everything looks grayer since you left.

You didn't break my wings,

but you left the sky without direction.

You didn't burn my memories,

but now they burn on their own inside me.

You were more than a loss:

you were an echo that won't stop,

a shadow that stays,

a *what if...* that still visits

when I close my eyes.

It wasn't what you did—

it was what you didn't do.

(UN)DONE

It wasn't the ending—

it was everything you promised before you left.

And even if it seems I've moved on,

there are parts of me still there,

in the silence,

in the dark,

in you.

When You Left

The clock didn't keep ticking,

even if the second hand pretended to move.

The leaves no longer fell the same,

the wind didn't sound like it used to.

The city went on with its noise,

but the world inside me

fell silent.

As if your absence

had pressed pause on my soul,

as if the echo of your footsteps

got stuck inside the walls.

Everything stopped—

except the memory of you.

That one keeps walking...

through my mind,

through my chest,

through the days

that no longer knows how to go on without you.

(UN)DONE

Life moved on,

but I...

I stayed in that day—

the day you left

and everything inside me

stayed behind with you.

What You Left Broken

I wish I could say this

to your face—

but some truths

are too heavy

to survive the silence between us.

You broke my heart

quietly,

like someone dropping a glass

and walking away

before it shatters.

You cracked the voice inside me

that once believed in herself,

and now every mirror

asks me:

who are you trying to be

if you're not enough for him?

You ruined my confidence.

Left it bleeding behind locked doors.

And now I'm here,

holding the pieces,

whispering to the child in me:

"How do I fix this?"

THE OPEN WOUND

Today I Choose

Today I decided
that in this life—
and in all the ones to come—
it will be you
who breaks my heart.

I choose you,
even if you hurt,
even if you never learn how to stay,
because even in your goodbyes
there's more truth
than in the arms of anyone else.

Maybe in another life,
we'll get it right.
Maybe next time,
you'll arrive on time.

But if not,
if everything repeats...
let it be you again—
the one who teaches me
how a heart breaks
without ever stopping
to love.

Not Letting Go

They told me: *let him go.*

But no one told me how.

No one said what to do

when the memory comes back—

with his scent,

his laughter,

his way of lingering

even after he's gone.

I try to sleep,

but in my mind, he's still speaking.

I try to forget,

but his name stuck

to my closed eyelids.

I don't want to keep loving

someone who's no longer here,

but my heart

hasn't gotten the memo that he's gone.

(UN)DONE

And here I am...

wanting not to feel,

but feeling everything.

Still You

Time passed.

The seasons changed—

and so did I.

I smiled again,

fell in love again,

let someone else trace

the edges you once kissed.

But I never stopped

looking for you

in the way they laughed,

in how they held my hand

without trembling.

I never stopped

thinking of you

in those quiet hours,

wondering if you still

feel me too

in the corners where love

no longer reaches.

(UN)DONE

And maybe

that's why it never works.

Maybe that's why

no one stays.

Because I keep trying

to build something new

on the ashes of a name

that still burns

softly

inside me.

Maybe you were the storm,

but also the calm.

And maybe—

just maybe—

it will never work

with anyone

who isn't

you.

No Subtlety

I don't want you to hurt me

gently,

or with hesitation.

I want you to destroy me completely—

no subtlety,

no empty promises.

Do it once and for all,

without mercy,

like someone ripping out by the root

what they never meant to plant.

The One

You make me question everything—

when your silence weighs more than your voice,

when your gestures no longer match

the memory I hold of you.

Am I in love with *you*,

or with the version of you I created myself?

The one who looked at me with tenderness,

the one who chose me without hesitation,

the one who maybe never existed...

except in my mind.

And it hurts.

It hurts not knowing

if I ever loved *you*,

or just the illusion I built

to keep from feeling alone.

No one else but you

It's not that no one wanted to stay—

it's that I didn't let them.

Because I don't want empty presences,

lukewarm hands,

or half-spoken promises.

I don't want anyone to stay...

not if it isn't you.

Because only you know

how to exist in my silence without shattering it,

how to look at my wounds

without asking for explanations.

And as long as it's not you,

I'll choose absence

over the kind of presence

that doesn't know how to love

The Summer That Never Came

We had so many plans

for next summer:

unhurried walks,

ice cream in the afternoon,

silly photos at sunset,

laughter anywhere.

We had promises

tucked into late-night talks,

dreams drawn with soft words,

and hearts that believed it all.

But that summer...

never came.

Not because of the sun,

or the season,

but because *you*

were gone

before the days grew long.

And now summer comes,

yes—

but it doesn't bring the same.

It no longer excites me.

It no longer hurts the same,

but it still hurts.

And every ray of sun

reminds me

that the summer I wanted most

remains

on pause.

You Left Without Breaking Me, And That Broke Me More

I never knew love could rot

while still blooming in my chest.

You touched my soul—

then left it bleeding,

as if it had never been yours to hold.

You didn't shatter me with cruelty,

you broke me with kindness.

With the way you vanished

softly,

like a ghost I had dreamed into flesh.

You never screamed.

You never fought.

You just... stopped choosing me.

And that quiet,

God, that silence,

ripped me apart more than any goodbye.

I was loving you

like a prayer whispered through cracked lips—

begging for a miracle

you never meant to give.

Now I live in the ruins

of all we never were,

haunted by the softness

you never meant as forever.

I never knew

that someone could leave

without leaving a mark—

and still

be the scar

that never lets me heal.

I Hate Myself

And I hate myself

for begging for a love

I don't deserve.

For kneeling my dignity

before crumbs of affection,

for staying where love

never grew roots.

I hate myself

for loving so fiercely

someone who barely saw me,

for giving all of me

to someone who only ever took parts.

And still—

even knowing it wasn't meant for me,

I stayed...

hoping it might hurt

just a little less.

Empty Hours

Everyone's out tonight—

laughing too loud,

drinking too much,

as if hearts didn't break

on weekends.

The city pulses

with people trying to forget,

while I sit here,

remembering everything.

My room feels too quiet,

but not in a peaceful way—

in the kind of silence

that hums with memories

and questions

that no one will ever answer.

I scroll through old photos

like someone searching for proof

that something once felt real.

(UN)DONE

It's 3:11 AM.

The streetlights flicker.

The world spins on.

And me?

I just sit

where you left me—

between the music outside

and the silence

that still has your name.

What the Fire Left Behind

All that remained were ruined cities,

streets where only memories walk,

bridges that lead nowhere,

and plazas where laughter burned out.

Your name was an echo that refused to die,

an ancient flame, always burning—

but I, I was only flesh,

a promise time was destined to corrupt.

You—endless—

didn't grow old with me.

Your eyes kept shining,

while mine grew dim,

like streetlamps in the rain.

I wanted to remain in your story,

to be a verse in your immortal memory,

but I was only a moment,

a heartbeat, a delay.

And in the end,

ruined cities were all that remained—

that's why an endless must never love an eternal:

Love hurts more

when it cannot die.

Selena Santos

I Wanted to Hold You,

I imagined your pain

so I could stay close—

so I had a reason

to wrap my arms around your silence

and pretend you needed saving.

I told myself

you were breaking,

so I wouldn't have to admit

you were just walking away.

I became the comfort

you never asked for,

the warmth

you never reached for.

And still,

I wanted to hold you—

not to fix you,

but to feel like I mattered.

Maybe you weren't hurting.

Maybe you just didn't want to stay.

68

But I needed your pain

to mean

something.

Because the truth is harder:

you didn't push me away

because you were broken.

You pushed me away

because you didn't love me

enough to hold on.

The Chair by the Window

There's a chair

by the window

that's still waiting.

No one moves it.

No one sits in it.

But every evening,

the sun touches the same side

as if it still believes

someone will return to fill it.

Its legs creak more now,

the wood has dulled,

and the cushion

has nearly forgotten its shape.

Still, it stays.

Stubborn.

Quiet.

Steady.

(UN)DONE

As if waiting were its only purpose.

As if remembering

were its way of loving.

And it's growing old — not from time, but from

absence, the kind that hollows wood.

Because some things

don't die from age—

they die of loneliness.

After Warmth

With you,

I forgot what winter felt like.

Your hands were fire,

your voice a blanket,

your presence—

a shelter

that made me believe

cold could never reach me again.

But now that you're gone,

I'm freezing.

dying.

Too much.

From the inside out.

The world didn't change,

but I no longer feel warmth.

You left me exposed

to a climate I no longer know how to survive.

And the worst part is,

without meaning to,

you also made me forget

what hell used to feel like.

Now I don't burn,

I only tremble.

And in that trembling—

I still look for you.

What We Almost Were.

And yes... on nights like this,

not even work,

nor noise,

nor exhaustion can save me.

I can fill every minute of the day,

bury myself in tasks,

in checklists,

in anything that keeps me from thinking.

But night comes

—as it always does—

and there you are,

sitting in my mind,

as if you never really left.

I miss what we used to be,

what we were,

what we almost were.

And it hurts to admit it:

I still think of you

when everything goes quiet.

Where Do You Go?

Where do you go

when the soul aches

and life feels like lead

pressing down on your chest?

When laughter sounds hollow,

and the echo of what once was

drowns out everything that is?

Where do broken dreams hide,

and hugs that never came,

and words that died

before they reached the lips?

I walk barefoot

across the scattered remains

of better days,

trying to remember

what it felt like to breathe

without fear,

to look at the sky

without wishing to fly away.

(UN)DONE

Where do you go

when your soul hurts

and life weighs more

than your body can carry?

Maybe to the corner

where we keep

the unsaid *I love yous,*

the goodbyes that never closed,

the silences

that hurt more than screams.

There I go...

aimless,

without a map,

chasing the shadow

of who I used to be—

hoping that, somewhere

in all this absence,

there's still a spark

that hasn't gone dark.

Dirac Knew it

It was already in the equation—

the existence of absence,

the antimatter of love,

the possibility of something felt

but never seen.

I was a particle,

you were the opposite.

And still,

when we collided,

we were a brief flash,

almost divine—

as if the universe

allowed its symmetry

to break just once.

I searched for you

in probabilities,

in every sign,

in every constant,

hoping that maybe,

just maybe,

the outcome would change.

But no.

It was written.

Like all beautiful tragedies,

like every formula

that can't be altered

without destroying

what makes it perfect.

And now that you're gone,

I'm left with physics—

the cold certainty

that everything that begins

is destined to decay.

And still…

I'd solve you again,

and again,

even if the answer is always

losing you.*

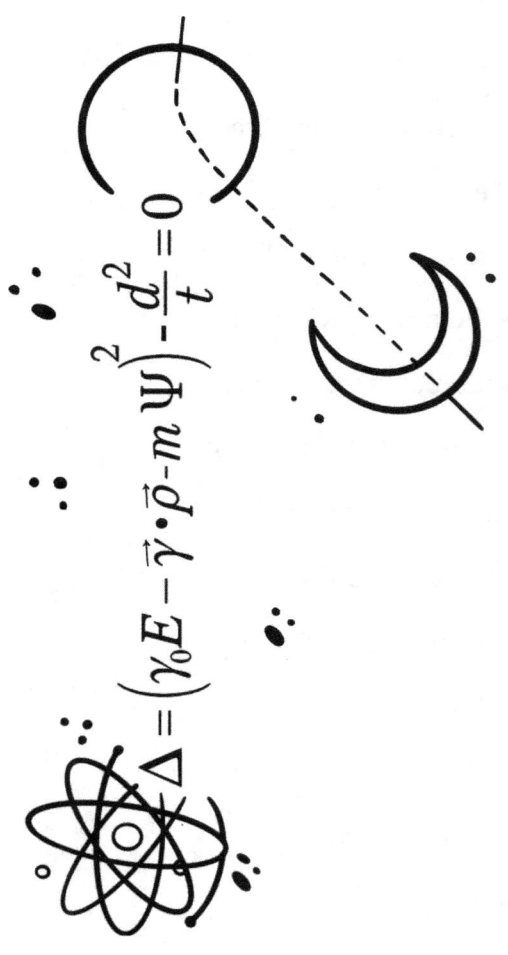

The Taste of You

How do I erase

the taste of you—

from my mouth,

from my dreams,

from my skin?

I've tried bitter coffee,

strangers' lips,

glasses poured too full,

but nothing

washes away

what you left behind.

You stayed

in the center of my tongue,

like a word left unspoken,

like a kiss that never fully landed.

What if it's not hunger anymore?

What if it's just memory?

Because even when I don't say your name,

I still taste you—

in every song, in every nameless night,

in every failed attempt

to forget.

How do I tear out a memory

shaped like your voice,

flavored like

what we used to be?

Cycles

I've been the one who hurts,

and the one who's left bleeding.

A walking wound—

sometimes in a kiss,

sometimes in the silence that follows.

I was shelter and storm.

A promise and a lie.

The one who whispered

 "stay" through fear,

and the one who walked away

without looking back,

even as my steps shook.

I've worn hugs like armor,

and words like thorns.

I met guilt the way we meet silence:

too late and unarmed.

I loved with a broken heart,

and broke what dared

to love me.

There's no redemption in this story—

only a trail of nights

where the names I never said

and the ones that were torn from me

still burn.

I've been the one who hurts,

and the one who's hurt.

And sometimes,

I don't know which version of me

I lost myself in.

Hard to Receive

Why is it so difficult

to love someone

who loves me?

Why do I flinch

at the softness?

Why does safety

feel like a trap,

and kindness

like a lie I don't deserve?

I say I want love—

but only chase the ones

who run.

I sabotage the arms

that stay open,

and drown in the silence

of the ones who don't.

Maybe it's not love

that I fear.

Maybe it's being truly seen—

without having to earn it,

without needing to bleed for it.

Why...

do I only know how to survive love,

but not live in it?

My Almost

We met at the wrong time—

when your hands had stopped reaching,

and mine already knew how to let go.

We looked at each other

like strangers who remember

something they never really had.

We were everything,

the soul longed for,

and everything

life refused to give.

We walked together

through a brief dream,

but morning returned us

to separate shores

of the same sadness.

You were my almost,

my maybe,

my not quite.

The story that screams in silence every time someone

asks if I've ever truly loved.

And how do I tell them

you still live in me—

in the songs I don't play,

in the places you're not,

in the hugs that never happened,

in the endings we never wrote?

We were...

what we never were.

Nothing

I don't feel anything.

Just this vast emptiness

stretching inside me

like an echo with no end.

I try to fill it—

with borrowed laughter,

with hugs that don't quite reach,

with people

even emptier than me.

But the hollow doesn't go away.

It just changes shape,

changes name,

wears a different face.

And sometimes I wonder

if the real problem

isn't the emptiness itself,

but my need

to hide it behind someone else

Selena Santos

instead of facing it

with me.

How Does Emptiness Feel?

Can someone explain to me

how I can feel so much

without feeling at all?

How my eyes fill with water

when there's no ocean,

how my soul trembles

with no wind,

how my chest aches

with no wound.

There are days

when silence feels heavy,

as if it were screaming,

and strangers' laughter

splits me

into invisible halves.

I walk.

I breathe.

I move.

But something in me

has stayed still.

Something cries

without sound.

Something longs

Without knowing for whom.

And it's there—

in that corner I can't name—

where I catch myself

feeling everything

without knowing

if I still feel anything at all.

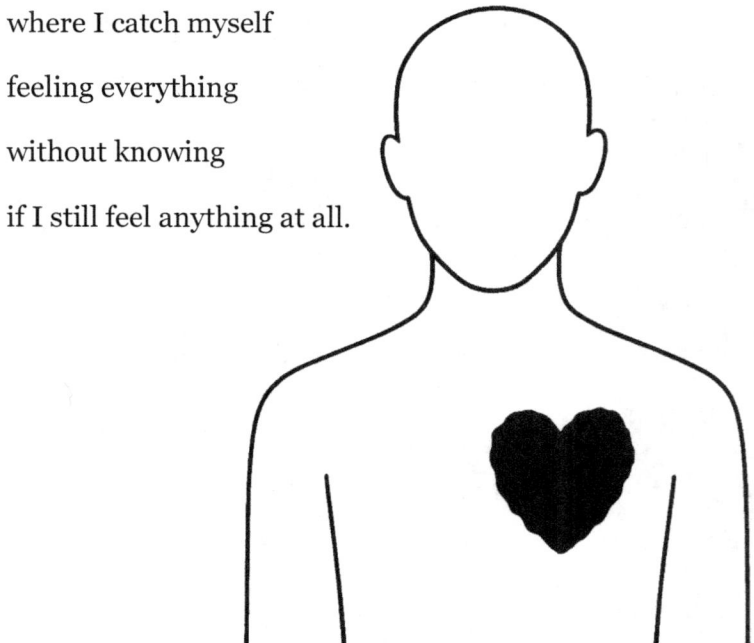

Architect of Silence

I've become an expert

at building homes

meant for solitude.

I know which corners

soften the echo,

which colors

feel like a hug,

and which windows

don't expect visitors.

I've learned

to pour two cups of coffee

and drink them both.

To speak softly,

so absence

doesn't get startled.

Loneliness never leaves—

it sits at the table,

settles in,

and sometimes—just sometimes—

reminds me

it isn't always punishment.

Sometimes,

it's refuge.

But there are nights

when it weighs more.

And even if the house feels full,

there's always one room

that echoes

I miss you.

No One Told My Heart

inspired by the song "Closure" by Hayd

I deleted the photos,

boxed up your letters,

even told my friends

"I'm fine now."

But no one told my heart

you're not coming back.

I tried to write an ending

to a story

you left mid-sentence.

Tried to close a door

that was never fully open.

I begged the silence

to mean something,

but it only echoed

your name back to me.

Maybe we would've been closer

if we were a couple years older—

less afraid,

more ready,

less lost.

There are questions in my head,

answers I won't get,

and every one of them

sounds like you.

I thought closure was something

I could create—

a ritual, a final word,

a deep breath

and a turning page.

But all I've found

is the ache

of unfinished love,

and the weight

of everything

you never stayed to answer.

Maybe I don't want closure.

Maybe I just wanted you

to care

enough to give me one.

Emergency Call

I dialed your name

like someone calling 911—

not out of habit,

but because I was collapsing.

My voice was a silent scream:

please answer—

there's still time.

But no one picked up.

Not you.

Not even the echo.

You were my structural failure,

my ground zero,

my before and after.

And I—

I stayed beneath the wreckage

of everything I imagined with you.

I called.

Once.

Twice.

Three times.

As if love had a direct line.

As if a code

could save us.

As if you hadn't already evacuated

before the fire even started.

Sometimes I wonder

if you heard the siren

and turned away,

or if you just silenced the alarm

because the disaster

wasn't yours to feel.

1-20-23

That was the number.

That was the day.

That was me:

calling for help,

and learning

that not every soul

Selena Santos

gets pulled from the ruins

in time.

Our Place

I went back.

To that corner where your laugh

once lingered on the walls,

and your shadow used to sleep

in the curve of the couch.

I wasn't alone this time.

She held my hand

the way you never could.

And still—

everything tasted like you.

The lights,

the low music,

the soft clink of glass against wood—

everything whispered your name

while I pretended to hear hers.

I smiled

with nostalgia clenched between my teeth,

like biting into a memory

that bleeds the soul

in silence.

You're gone,

and yet you're everywhere—

in the place,

in my unfocused gaze,

in the silence

stretching between her words

and the version of you

I still imagine replying.

I came back...

this time,

to understand

that some places

aren't ours anymore—

even if we're still shattered

inside them.

Heavy Sadness

It's not exhaustion.

It's sadness

that moved in quietly

and never left.

The kind that doesn't scream,

but weighs.

The kind

you can't explain to anyone

because they wouldn't know what to say—

because saying it

would only make it hurt more.

And it's fucking me up.

Carrying all of this

inside

with nowhere to put it.

It's fucking me up

not having you.

Your absence burns in my chest

like something that won't heal,

like something that returns

every single day.

I'm not tired.

I'm broken—

and full

of everything

I never said.

Miss Me

Miss me,

please.

Do it—

even if it's just a bit.

Even if it's only in silence,

only at night,

only when something small reminds you of me.

Miss me—

But do it,

not out of guilt.

Not out of habit.

But because part of you

still remembers

how it felt when we didn't feel so far.

False Prophet

I thought you were heaven-sent—

arriving with that quiet calm,

those soft words

that almost sounded like salvation.

You hid your wings well.

You smiled like grace,

touched me like peace,

and I, so tired of falling,

mistook you for a place to land.

But I crashed.

Hard.

With belief still clinging to my bones,

with the ache of someone

who'd never known how to fly,

but jumped anyway.

You were only human—

the kind that speaks of forever

with one foot out the door,

that holds you with arms

but not with soul.

Still, sometimes,

I look to the clouds,

hoping to find a glimpse of you—

though I know

even God

wouldn't call you His.

I thought I had found an angel...

but you were just the echo

of every prayer I whispered

when I was too broken

to pray out loud.

I Didn't Know

I didn't know

that silence could echo like that—

your name bouncing off the walls

of a heart

that still remembers the sound of you.

I didn't know

that goodbyes

don't always come with closure,

sometimes they just

linger

like perfume

on clothes you no longer wear.

I didn't know

how deep love had grown,

until I tried to pull it out—

and found roots tangled in my bones.

I didn't know

how much I needed you

until your absence

became a constant presence.

Now I'm left

counting what I never said,

writing poems for the ghost of your touch,

and learning

too late—

that I never knew

how to love you

until you were

already gone.

Not in This Life

I love how safe she makes me feel.

The way she makes my heart race.

How her laughter loosens my fears,

how her presence silences my storms,

how just *being there*

reminds me that tenderness still exists in this world.

And—damn it—I've fallen in love...

I've fallen in love with the woman of my life.

But not in this one.

In this life,

timing is off,

distances are heavy,

and old wounds rule everything.

In this life,

we are not what we could have been.

Maybe in another—

we'd find each other without urgency,

without excuses,

without fear.

(UN)DONE

Maybe in another,

she could stay too.

But in this one...

We met too late.

And though I loved her with all the love I knew how to

give—

this life didn't know how to hold us.

In a Parallel World

In a parallel world,

our lives align—

like trains that never miss their crossing,

like glances that always arrive on time.

There, your hands never let go of mine,

and my silences don't scare you.

There, time doesn't work against us,

and pride never forces us into silence.

In that other world,

I find you without searching,

and you stay without breaking promises.

We laugh with no expiration date.

Sometimes I close my eyes

and walk through that imagined place—

where we were never strangers,

where we never said goodbye.

But I wake up...

and here, in this world that never was,

(UN)DONE

I'm left with one certainty:

that somewhere,

 in some universe,

you miss me too.

I Went Back to Our Place

I went back to our place,

but this time, your hand wasn't in mine.

A different name, a different laugh—

and yet, you were everywhere.

The breeze smelled like your silences.

The lights flickered like your eyes

when you used to say this was something rare,

like the universe was watching us from the corner of

its eye.

I walked past where we used to laugh,

but I didn't laugh this time.

Because in every shadow, on every bench—

it was you.

You, without being there.

I wanted to talk about the food,

about that coffee we never liked,

but the words stayed in my throat.

Because it wasn't you beside me.

(UN)DONE

Funny how I came back with someone else,

and still felt alone.

Because the place is still ours,

even if we no longer are.

Among Sunflowers

I found myself among sunflowers,

searching for you in every sunbeam

that brushed my shoulders

like your hands once did

when you still remembered how to love me.

The field was quiet,

but inside me,

everything screamed your name.

The flowers turned toward the sun,

and I—foolish—

kept turning toward your memory.

They say sunflowers don't choose,

they just follow the light...

and maybe that's why I never left,

because your absence

still shone inside me.

There, among golden stalks and open skies,

I learned

that the hardest part isn't losing someone,

(UN)DONE

but blooming

with their shadow still rooted in you.

Among sunflowers,

I learned to face the light

with tears in my eyes,

to smile without reason,

and to carry you

without ever saying your name.

Neurochemistry

We were serotonin and dopamine:

the perfect mix of balance and bliss—

a biochemical spark

between your laugh

and my stillness.

I was the steady pulse,

the one who calmed your inner storms.

You were the flash of chaos

that made me feel alive,

even when I didn't know why.

We didn't quite function apart.

Your absence was a chemical crash,

my distance, a fading signal.

The body knew,

the soul screamed it—

we were incomplete without each other.

We needed one another

like the limbic system needs a heartbeat,

like breath needs a brain to remember.

(UN)DONE

We were chemical chaos,

but together...

almost human.

And now that you're gone,

my levels collapse.

Everything fades to gray,

as if science itself

can't explain

why some bodies,

when pulled apart,

start to break.

We were—

two silhouettes linked by synapses,

with serotonin and dopamine

still floating

between the silence.

Your Eyes

You look at me

as if I still lived in you,

as if you missed my hands,

as if my name hurt in silence.

 And for a moment,

I believe it too.

For a second,

I forget that love isn't measured by glances,

but by presence,

by action,

by staying.

Because if you truly loved me,

it wouldn't be your eyes saying so,

but your steps.

And since you don't come,

since you don't call,

since you don't fight...

today I choose

to believe your silence.

Not because it doesn't hurt,

but because I finally understand

that some eyes burn with fire

and still

leave you in the dark.

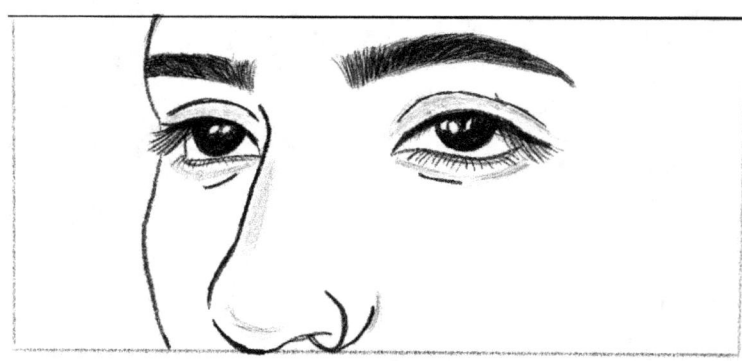

The Rains of June

I had forgotten the rains of June,

the ones that smell like wet earth and goodbyes,

the ones that carry in their drops

the echoes of what we once were.

They came back today, suddenly,

tapping on the window like you used to—

with that sweetness that foretold a storm

but also promised shelter.

And I caught myself looking for you

in every puddle that mirrored the sky,

as if your shadow still knew

how to walk beside me.

How strange...

you think you've healed,

until it rains,

until the calendar says June again.

And there you are—

not in flesh, not in voice,

but in that soft kind of longing

that only rain can bring

when all that's left is to remember.

I had forgotten the rains of June...

but not you.

Go

Go on, be happy—

You there, and me here.

You with her,

and me without you.

Meanwhile,

I'll pretend I don't miss you.

And who knows...

Maybe if I pretend long enough,

it'll start to feel true.

Not Even Then

I've emptied every bottle,

chasing your absence in sips that taste like nothing.

I've danced with shadows in strangers' rooms,

screaming your name in languages I don't

understand.

Not drunk,

not lost in lights that flicker like your lies,

not drowning in laughter that doesn't belong to me—

not even then can I stop thinking of you.

I've brushed delirium,

mixing tears with psychedelia,

begging some parallel universe

to teach me how to live without you.

But even in my most shattered state,

even with my mind hanging from the ceiling,

even when the world spins and I can't keep up—

you stay.

You are that filthy, recurring,

sick thought...

the kind no sweet poison can erase.

And it hurts.

Because no drug is more addictive

than the memory of you.

And not even like this,

not this far from myself,

you stop hurting me.

Still Here

I don't look for you,

but I find you—

in the pause between songs,

in the curl of coffee steam,

in the silences I make

when I don't know what to think.

I let you go long ago,

with trembling hands

and a soul shattered

like someone missing a train

they know won't ever return.

And still,

you live in my mind

like a guest who never left,

like a shadow

that learned its way back.

24/7.

You're there.

In dreams that don't call for you

but still summon your name,

in phrases I repeat

as if they once belonged to you.

I don't know why you're still here,

not when I no longer wait for you,

not when I no longer love you

(at least not like before).

But I get it now:

you were so deep

that even without meaning to,

my mind still whispers your name

when everything else goes quiet.

Unfinished Connection.

Some people

arrive at the perfect moment

with souls out of sync.

Stories that brush against each other

but never get written.

Glances that promise

but never deliver.

Connections...

that never connected.

We understood each other in silence,

read between the lines,

but something—

something invisible and cruel—

kept us apart,

even when we were close.

And so we remained:

two perfect pieces

from different puzzles.

An attempt

that never knew how to begin

but still

hurt when it ended.

I don't know if you were

a mistake in timing

or a lesson in disguise.

I only know

we were an unfinished connection.

And that—

even without a name—

is something you feel

forever.

Root in the Air

What if that was the beginning

of something we never let grow?

A trembling seed in the palm,

waiting for soil,

but we left

before planting.

We had the spark,

but not the flame.

The glance,

but not the step.

The want,

but not the time.

And still...

I think of you

like one thinks of what could've been—

not with anger,

but with a tenderness

that aches a little.

(UN)DONE

Maybe we weren't a love,

but we were a possibility.

And that—that too takes root,

even if only

in the air.

What If

I was left

wanting to know

what would happen if...

If you had stayed

five minutes longer.

If you had said

what your eyes almost confessed.

If I had reached out

one last time

instead of letting silence

settle between us

like dust on a forgotten photograph.

What would've happened

if we hadn't been so afraid—

of timing,

of truth,

of the weight of our own hearts?

I still carry the questions

like unopened letters,

sealed with things

we never said.

And maybe

that's the cruelest part of it all:

not that you left,

but that you left

before the story

ever had a chance

to begin.

I was left

wanting to know

what would happen if...

And I'll never know.

Van Gogh

As beautiful

as the ruins of Troy—

devastated,

burning with memory,

each stone echoing

a story no one forgets.

Or maybe...

as beautiful

as Van Gogh's skies:

stormy,

wild,

colors screaming

what the soul couldn't silence.

I don't know if you were war or art,

flame or brushstroke,

but I swear—

there was something in you

that hurt and dazzled at once.

(UN)DONE

And I—

without armor or canvas,

stood there

watching you burn

softly.

Like a Book

You were

like that book so good

you don't want it to end—

but you just can't stop reading.

Every page with you

was a sigh,

a surprise,

a knot in my chest.

You said things

that felt like underlines

on the pages of my soul.

And I,

addicted to your story,

kept reading

even knowing

the ending would hurt.

I didn't want it to finish,

but I needed to know

how we ended.

(UN)DONE

And when I turned the last page,

there was no explosion,

no perfect closing line—

just silence.

And that hollow feeling

left by books

that become a part of you.

Love of My Life

Forgive me for letting you go.

Forgive me

for not knowing how to hold on

when all I wanted

was to hold you forever.

It hurts.

God, how it hurts!

Because I let you go

with trembling hands

and a heart screaming not to.

But I did.

And since then,

everything feels heavier.

I was a coward.

I thought it was better to walk away

before I failed you—

and in the end,

I failed you by not staying.

(UN)DONE

You were peace in the chaos,

You were home,

shelter,

life.

And I closed the door.

Out of fear.

Out of clumsiness.

Out of not knowing

how to love something so real.

I never stopped loving you.

Not for a single day.

I think of you in every silence,

cry for you in every long night.

And no matter how well I pretend,

no one will ever know

how broken I've been

since you left.

I wish you knew—

that I still love you

with a fire that burns

even if no one sees it.

You were the love of my life.

You are.

You always will be.

And if you ever came back,

I swear this time

I would fight with everything

I didn't have before.

But if you don't...

if it's too late,

if you're already in someone else's arms—

at least let me say this:

I carry you in me

like someone carries a ghost

they loved too much.

And even if it hurts,

even if it destroys me...

I'll go on loving you

until my final breath.

— 02:18

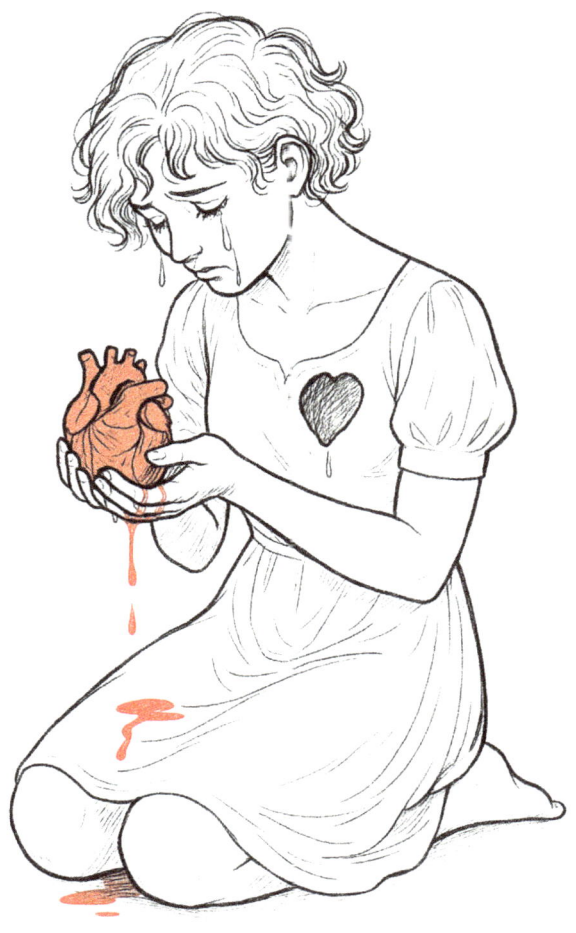

Idealization

You make me wonder:

Am I in love with *you*?

Or with the version of you

I built in my mind?

The one who looked at me differently,

who said exactly what I needed to hear,

who stayed

when everything hurts.

Do I love *you*...

or who I imagined you could be?

Do I miss *you*...

or the shelter I created in your name?

Maybe you were never

who I wanted to believe.

And maybe,

I just needed to love someone—

even if it was only an idea.

And What Will Happen?

And what will happen to all the plans we made?

To the trips born in warm late-night talks.

The promises whispered between yawns and laughter.

The names of the children will never have?

Where do the songs we chose together go,

the coffees we left for later,

the streets we swore we'd walk hand in hand

as if the world couldn't break us?

Tell me, where are futures that never happened kept?

Who gathers the dreams when they fall to the floor

and no one stays behind to sweep them up?

I don't know

if you still think of them,

if closing your eyes still hurts

with everything

we never got to live.

But I...

I keep finding them

in every silence.

Solitude

Solitude, by itself, isn't wrong.

There's peace in being with yourself,

a silence that doesn't scream,

a presence that doesn't hurt.

What hurts

is feeling alone when you're by yourself.

Empty in your own body.

A stranger in your own skin.

That's where something breaks.

That's when solitude stops being company

and becomes echo.

A shadow.

A wound.

Because being alone

is not the same

as not knowing how to live within yourself.

3:00 A.M.

I stayed awake

until 3:00 a.m.

waiting for a message—

something simple,

like "I'll sleep with you."

Not in the literal way,

but the kind that says,

"you're not alone."

The kind that promises

to sit with the silence.

I checked my phone

more times than I'll admit,

as if a notification

could patch the hole

you left behind.

But nothing came.

Not your message,

not your voice,

not that invisible warmth

you used to carry.

Only the ceiling,

the insomnia,

and this foolish hope

that just once—

you might choose to stay.

In You

Life knows

where to hit the hardest.

It doesn't warn,

doesn't ask,

doesn't hesitate.

And me...

it hit me

right in you.

In the way you left

as if you weren't everything.

In your silence,

louder than any scream.

In how you turned my days

into nothing,

and my nights

into everything you were.

It could've hurt

in a thousand other places,

but it chose

your name.

Your laugh I still hear,

your eyes that no longer see me,

your memory

that stayed

even when you didn't.

Life was precise.

And it broke me...

right in you.

Where Does Sadness Go

How do you pull out

all the sadness

you carry inside?

The kind that doesn't cry—

it just weighs.

That stays

when everyone else leaves.

That doesn't scream,

but won't let you sleep either.

Do you cry it out?

Write it down?

Seal it in jars

and forget it in a drawer somewhere?

And where do *you* go

when you no longer want to be here?

When the body keeps going

but the soul

is searching for an exit.

When breathing

is more habit

than desire.

Maybe there's no answer.

Just moments

where it hurts a little less.

Brief flickers of light

within the knot.

Maybe it doesn't go.

Maybe you learn

to live with the weight.

And still,

someday—hopefully—

it'll hurt less.

Flores

He gave me petals,

soft and sweet,

but never mentioned

how deeply they could bleed.

I took them with open hands,

with my heart uncovered,

believing that love

didn't hurt

if it was real.

And it hurts.

He offered flowers

then silence.

Promises

then distance.

The thorns weren't in the bouquet—

they were in the way he loved.

In gestures that cut,

in words that wounded

without ever raising their voice.

I still keep the flowers,

wilted,

their thorns untouched.

Reminding me

that not everything that blooms

can be held

without bleeding.

Eyes Don't Lie

The worst part of disappointment

isn't just the sleepless nights—

it's not even being able to cry.

The tears won't come,

but I feel it...

I feel it in my tired eyes,

in the weight behind my smile

that doesn't quite reach them.

Because some truths

aren't spoken out loud,

they live quietly

in the eyes that whisper,

"I'm not okay."

The Shape of My Fears

I was afraid you would hurt me.

But you mercilessly destroyed me completely.

I tiptoed around your silences,

read between your pauses,

held my breath

each time you pulled away—

hoping you'd come back

Softer

But love—

you returned like a storm.

Not sudden, just unstoppable.

And I,

so willing to forgive the thunder,

ignored the flood.

You didn't just bruise me—

you unmade me.

(UN)DONE

Word by word,

touch by touch,

until nothing of who I was

felt like mine anymore.

I feared the ache

of being left behind...

but nothing compares

to being forgotten

while still holding on.

And now,

I sleep beside my wounds,

call them by your name,

and wonder if you ever felt

a fraction of the breaking

you caused.

You tried

How do you fix

what you didn't break?

How do you stitch a soul

that others left in pieces?

I came to you

like an abandoned house—

shattered windows,

hallways still echoing

with old screams.

You weren't to blame,

but you paid the price

for loving someone

still afraid to be loved.

And it's unfair.

So cruelly unfair

that your tenderness had to fight

ghosts you never met,

that your embrace faced a cold

you didn't cause.

You tried everything.

And I...

I only knew how to shut down.

I'm sorry.

Not for leaving,

but for arriving so broken

and expecting *you*

to teach me

how not to hurt.

—12:28

Unsurpassable

How do you move on

from someone who was both sky and storm,

who lived inside you

without ever touching your skin?

How do you forget

someone who reached your soul

before your body?

How do you erase

the exact way they said your name,

like it was

the only word that ever mattered?

Some absences can't be filled—

not with books,

not with bodies,

not with shiny new promises.

Some people are unsurpassable

because they weren't meant to be replaced,

but to carve a before and after

into your weary soul.

(UN)DONE

And no, maybe you never move on.

Maybe you just learn

to live with the hollow,

to smile through the wound,

to keep walking

even when the goodbye still aches.

Liquid Silence

I wanted to get drunk

to get rid of that lump in my throat—

the one made of words

I never said,

goodbyes I swallowed,

and memories

that still sting like fresh cuts.

So I poured another glass,

hoping it would blur your name,

drown your echo,

soften the edges

of the night you walked away.

But alcohol doesn't heal—

it just delays the bleeding.

And somewhere between sips and silence,

I found myself

drunk on everything

I never got to tell you.

I laughed louder,

just to quiet the ache.

I danced slower,

just to feel something

that wasn't regret.

And still,

there you were—

in every shadow,

in every drop,

in every version of myself

that misses you

more than I should.

I wanted to get drunk

to forget,

but all I did

was remember

more clearly.

I Did It Again

I did it again.

I re-read our old messages,

and I miss that person you were.

I miss you

like you have no fucking idea.

I scrolled through words

that once felt like home,

like proof

that we had something real—

something worth holding onto.

You said you cared.

You said forever.

And I believed every syllable

like it was scripture.

Now, your name feels foreign

on my tongue,

but your memory—

it still lives in my chest,

ruthless and uninvited.

(UN)DONE

I miss the way you used to see me,

like I was enough,

like I was yours.

Before the cold,

before the distance,

before you turned into

someone I wouldn't recognize

if we passed on the street.

But the worst part?

I don't just miss the past—

I miss who I was

when I believed

you meant it.

That's the Matter

Sometimes the only thing that I need

is a hug.

That's it.

Nothing more.

Just arms around me

tight enough

to quiet the storm

spinning in my chest.

But—

a hug from a specific person.

That's the matter.

Because not all hugs

feel like home.

Not all hands

know how to hold

what's breaking without a sound.

I don't need comfort

from just anyone.

I need yours.

(UN)DONE

The way you used to pull me in

like you knew

I was falling apart

even when I smiled.

And now,

on the loneliest nights,

when everything feels too loud

and too quiet at once,

I realize—

it was never just the hug I needed.

It was you...

That's the matter.

For Real

I hope one day

you can love me

for real.

Not just in the quiet hours

when no one's watching.

Not just in whispers,

or in almosts,

or in the way your eyes

search for me

but your hands never stay.

I hope one day

you look at me

and don't flinch

at the depth of what I feel,

don't run

from the softness

you once said you admired.

Because I've loved you

without holding back—

(UN)DONE

in silence,

in distance,

in dreams that still

wake me up at 3 a.m.

with your name

like a bruise on my chest.

But I know

you never truly chose me.

You held me close,

but not completely.

You said you cared,

but not entirely.

So I hope—

one day,

when the world feels quieter,

when your heart's no longer afraid—

you can love me

for real.

Even if by then,

it's too late.

Still Echoes

Your memories

still hit me

every now and then.

Not like a storm—

not anymore.

More like a breeze

that carries your name

into a quiet room

where I thought

I had finally forgotten.

It happens

in songs we used to love,

in places we never got to visit,

in words I hear

that sound too much

like something you'd say.

And suddenly,

I'm there again—

missing you

(UN)DONE

in a thousand silent ways.

I smile less

and remember more.

And for a moment,

it all feels close again.

Too close.

Your memories

still hit me

every now and then.

Not to break me—

just to remind me

that healing doesn't mean

forgetting.

I Never Thought I'd Miss You Like This

I never thought your silence

would echo louder than your voice.

That a goodbye never said

could break me more than the loudest scream.

You touched me in ways

I didn't know could bruise.

Not with hands—

but with absence,

with memories you left stitched to my skin.

I gave you all the light I had

and still,

you walked away

like it never warmed you.

Now I sit in rooms we never shared,

feeling the weight

of every laugh we might've had.

I never knew love could vanish

while still burning inside me.

I never knew forgetting

could feel like betrayal

to my own heart.

And still—

I whisper your name

like it's a prayer

I no longer believe in

Everything eventually ends

Today, you hurt like hell.

Tomorrow, it'll hurt the same.

By Wednesday, it'll be bearable.

Thursday, I'll remember you kindly.

Friday, you'll think of me.

By Saturday, I'll have forgotten you.

And on Sunday, you'll come back—

but by then,

it will all be over.

SUTURE

Don't Make Me Do It Quick

I'm afraid

of leaving you behind

when I get tired of all this.

And I'm afraid for you—

because I know

you are going to fall apart.

You always do.

Every time I step back,

even just a little,

your world cracks

like glass under pressure.

But I'm not made of glue.

I can't keep holding together

what doesn't want

to stay whole.

And still—

I care.

Still,

I hesitate.

(UN)DONE

Still,

I stay.

One more day.

One more fight.

One more version of pretending

we're not already breaking.

Don't make me do it quickly.

Don't make me become

the villain

in your story.

Don't wait until I'm empty

to finally listen.

Because when I go—

really go—

I won't look back.

And you'll be left

trying to piece yourself together

with hands

that never learned

how to hold me right.

Pretty Face

He had beautiful brown eyes,

eyes that seemed to know about love.

Lips the color of lies,

that knew exactly where to touch to wound...

A porcelain smile

—fragile, perfect, dangerous—

But that was all he was—

just a *pretty face*,

with recycled words

and a heart stuck in airplane mode.

You wrapped yourself in compliments

like bait on a hook,

waiting for someone like me

to bite the illusion.

And I did.

I fell.

I believed.

But the glow fades

when there's no soul behind the eyes,

(UN)DONE

no truth in the smile,

no intent to care for what you touch.

He was a perfect portrait

for a gallery of mistakes:

beautiful from afar,

empty up close.

And I learned—

that a pretty face

doesn't always mean a soul worth loving.

The Most Beautiful Demon

He looks at me

as if I were the most beautiful demon

he's ever seen—

a creature made of fire and longing,

with sharpened edges

and gentle eyes.

He's not afraid of my darkness.

He traces it with his gaze.

He studies it

like art that shouldn't exist,

but somehow it does.

In his eyes,

I'm not something to be feared,

but something

meant to be understood.

Unwrapped.

Worshipped.

Even if it burns.

And for a moment,

I believe him.

I believe I can be ruin and wonder all at once—

and still

be loved.

Scattered Papers

Some days,

life feels like a cluttered desk:

unpaid bills,

half-finished coffees,

and post-its screaming broken promises.

Hours crash into keystrokes,

emails arrive without mercy,

and the clock—that punctual tyrant—

mocks us with every tick

for all we couldn't finish.

Tasks pile up

like thoughts with nowhere to go,

and in the noise of routine,

we forget to breathe,

we forget to feel.

But even in the chaos,

there is beauty too:

a sudden laugh,

a sunbeam resting on the desk,

the quiet hope that,

even when everything is out of place,

sometimes,

A mess is a kind of home too.

O.K.

I'm not happy,

but I'm not sad either.

I still have trouble sleeping,

but I can handle it now.

The wounds you left

don't hurt as much anymore.

I guess that's what they meant

when they said I'd heal.

Healing.

I'm healing.

But you'll leave traces...

I'll always carry traces of you.

Music

Some people

stay in the music,

not in your life.

And that's okay.

Because at least there,

they always sound sweet.

And that's the beautiful—

and painful—thing about songs:

they keep speaking

even when the words no longer do.

You got trapped in those melodies.

Selena Santos

You remain tangled in those melodies.

Take It All

Take all the memories.

Take them and leave nothing.

Not laughter,

not photos,

not words that still hurt when it rains.

I don't want to keep

the crumbs of what we were,

or the shadow

of what we never became.

I don't want your voice

echoing in my head

when everything else is quiet.

I don't want your ghost-hands

haunting my tired skin.

Take even the echo.

Even the air

we once shared.

And if you can,

take the thought, too—

the one that says

 this could've ended differently.

Today, I'm not keeping you.

Today, I'm letting you go.

Completely.

Countless

There have been countless nights

when I went to sleep

wishing I wouldn't wake up.

Countless times I looked in the mirror

and hated what I saw.

Countless moments I gave up...

even if only on the inside.

But there was something—

something that kept me from letting go of it all.

Today I understand:

that something was me,

screaming in silence

not to give up,

to hold on just a little longer,

to believe I was still worth the fight,

even when everything hurts.

Cross-Contamination

I analyzed you like a pure sample,

but I never read the warning label.

I brought you into my sterile zone—

no gloves, no protocol—

trusting you wouldn't leave behind residue.

But you were reactive.

A contaminant

in my most vulnerable processes.

There was an error in measuring affection,

and my results came back as false positives:

I thought you loved me.

I tried to centrifuge your absences,

to separate them from care,

but everything settled at the bottom

like a precipitate of something no longer useful.

I searched for you in every spectrum of light,

logged you in my emotional records,

until the system crashed:

overload of promises,

reciprocity deficiency.

Now I'm a broken sample,

with values outside the reference range.

And you...

just a lab error

I won't make again.

In a Hurry, yet composed

I move with urgency,

but with calm—

like someone who wants to arrive

without missing the journey.

Like someone who's cried so much

that now, they just want to breathe

without it hurting.

I'm in a rush for peace,

but I won't force it.

I've learned that good things

don't always arrive shouting—

Sometimes they whisper.

I walk fast,

but I'm not running away.

I no longer flee,

I search.

And if I stumble,

I don't punish myself:

I pause.

I breathe.

And I rise again.

In a hurry to live,

with calm to feel.

Because I finally understood—

it's not about getting there first,

but not losing myself

along the way.

Don't Come Back

Please don't come back.

Don't come back with that smile

to which it is impossible for me to say no.

Don't bring your soft words,

or that gaze that undresses me without touch.

Don't tempt me.

Don't look at me like that.

Don't seduce me—

I might fall again.

Don't speak

as if you never left.

Because you know it.

I might believe you again.

I might love you again.

I might fall again.

Don't come back—

it's taken me so long

to learn how to sleep

with the lights off after you.

(UN)DONE

And I don't want

to fear the dark again.

With My Soul in My Hands

I arrived like this:

with my soul in my hands,

trembling,

like someone offering something

that's been broken many times

but still believes it has worth.

I didn't bring flowers,

or excuses,

or shiny promises.

Just this part of me—

as fragile as it is honest,

as tired as it is alive.

I showed it to you without decoration,

without filters,

without armor.

And for the first time,

I wasn't afraid of the pain.

Because I understood

there's a quiet beauty

196

in holding what's left of you

after the collapse,

and still

offering it with tenderness.

With my soul in my hands,

I chose myself.

And finally knew

I don't need to be perfect

to be real.

After So Much

After so much,

you learn to see

each sunrise

as a blank canvas,

a new forgiveness,

a truce for the soul.

You learn to leave behind

the guilt that was never yours,

to walk lighter,

to breathe without fear.

Because after so much,

you no longer live out of habit—

you live by choice.

And each day

is a chance

to return to yourself.

Your Own First

First, you have to break your own heart—

not out of spite,

but out of understanding.

To know

what the abyss feels like,

how absence burns,

how one rebuilds oneself after being lost.

No one heals without first breaking,

no one truly loves

without first having failed oneself.

Monday

After everything,

you no longer wait anxiously for the weekends.

You learn to get along with Sunday afternoons.

And you no longer hate Mondays.

After everything,

you learn to see each day

as a new chance

for something better,

something different,

something that changes you.

And it happens.

One day, your life changes,

and you realize

you spent too much time

hating Mondays,

without knowing

that one day, they'd become your favorite.

And you love them now,

because finally you understand—

(UN)DONE

Monday was never the problem.

It was the weight you brought into it.

Reconstruction

I'm repairing what others broke in me.

Gently picking up

the pieces they left scattered,

patiently mending

the cracks they once called flaws.

And you should see...

how beautiful I'm becoming.

Stronger,

softer,

more mine.

I don't shine like I used to—

I shine differently.

Now my light comes from within,

from everything I learned

while learning to rise again.

Unhurried

I finally understood.

I'm no longer in a rush.

I don't need to arrive first,

nor prove that I've stopped hurting.

I don't have to be okay every day,

or explain why my hands still tremble

when someone hugs me too tightly.

I've learned to inhabit myself.

To walk slowly within me

without tripping over the ruins.

I've stopped looking for answers

in other people's cracks,

and started planting calm

on my own.

It didn't happen suddenly,

or with a click,

or some magic phrase.

It was a slow process—

like light slipping in through a forgotten window.

I finally understood.

I'm no longer in a rush.

Because healing isn't about running,

it's about staying.

And this time,

I'm staying with me.

It Still Hurts Sometimes

Your memories

still hit me

every now and then.

Not like before—

not like a scream,

not like an open wound.

Now they're more like

offbeat heartbeats,

sighs I didn't plan,

glances that drift

without knowing why.

I thought you didn't hurt anymore.

And it's true...

not everything hurts now.

But sometimes,

in certain places,

with certain songs,

there are parts of me

that still remember you

205

as if you never left.

And it's not that I miss you.

It's just that some memories

take longer to leave

than people do.

And that's okay.

Because each time you hurt,

you hurt less.

And I...

I hold myself tighter.

Invisible Melody

Sometimes,

sad music holds the pain no one else sees,

gently touches scars no one asks about,

puts into melody

what you don't know how to say,

and in every note, it whispers

what your voice has kept quiet for far too long.

It's not masochism—

it's refuge.

It's letting the echo of other broken hearts

tell you: "you're not alone."

Because there's beauty in sadness

when it isn't hidden,

when it's felt without fear,

when it slow-dances with your shadows

and doesn't ask you to heal too soon.

And yes, crying to a song

sometimes hurts less

than staying silent.

If I Could Hurt for You

If I could open my chest and make you a refuge,

I'd break every rib

just to shelter you.

If I could tear the weight from your soul,

I'd carry your cross without hesitating

 a single heartbeat.

 I would take the pain for you,

like one who drinks poison

 knowing there's no cure.

I'd walk your moonless nights,

and lose myself in your abyss

just so you could escape.

Give me your tears—

I'll make them mine.

Give me your screams—

I'll swallow them in silence.

Let me bleed

 what you don't want to feel,

let me cry

what would shatter you.

Because even if you never ask for anything,

even if you walk away without looking back,

my love needs no reason to burn:

I would hurt for you...

without you noticing,

Never close enough to reach you—

I would hurt for you

—Mom

(UN)DONE

Suture

You left me open,

like a surgical wound left unclosed,

with my pericardium exposed

and my soul bleeding out.

I tried emotional compression,

applied doses of forgetting every eight hours,

but the memory was resistant—

like a bacteria with no cure.

Your words, scalpel in hand,

made incisions where it already hurt.

No anesthesia was enough,

no suture held without breaking into sobs.

You were my chronic trauma,

my diagnosis with no treatment,

an arrhythmia that wouldn't stabilize,

a pain that felt like the chest...

but was born in the soul.

Now, all I can do is heal slowly,

close with thread what you opened with fire,

and let time,

like a skilled surgeon,

rebuild me...

without you.

11-12

We don't share the same blood.

but you cared for me

as if we did.

You taught me to love without conditions,

without demands,

without needing to be near.

To love through gestures,

through silence,

through the heart.

You were warmth

when I didn't know I was cold.

You were a guide

without even trying.

And without meaning to,

you showed me the kind of mother

I want to be someday—

one who embraces with her soul,

who leaves invisible footprints,

who doesn't need to be present

to still remain.

Now I carry your date on my skin:

as a promise,

as a memory,

as a lighthouse.

Because some people

don't leave.

They simply become

light.

For When You Tremble

If your heart trembles today,

don't stop it.

Don't silence it.

Let it speak.

Sometimes nerves aren't weakness,

but your body's way of reminding you

that you're stepping through a door

you once only admired from afar.

Breathe.

You're not failing.

You're feeling.

And that alone is an act of courage.

You don't need to have it all figured out,

or smile if you can't.

Just stay.

With yourself.

In yourself.

Like someone who holds themselves

even while shaking,

215

like someone who chooses themselves

even without knowing

how long the pain will last.

Today you're here.

And that...

That is already more than enough.

Anatomy of Pain

Pain has bones.

It creaks in your chest when you breathe deep,

settles between your ribs

like a guest who never asked to stay.

It has veins,

flows through the blood in the form of memories,

wraps around your throat

and speaks with the trembling voice of all that was

never said.

Pain has skin.

The kind that burns without being touched,

that bristles at absence,

that misses even what once hurt.

It has eyes,

but they always look inward,

toward the exact hollow

where hope used to beat.

And it has memory.

One that doesn't forget,

that replays scenes as if reliving them

were the only way to understand.

This is its anatomy:

it doesn't live in one part of the body—

it lives in all of you.

And still, there are days—few, slow, luminous—

when it feels lighter.

Not because it's gone,

but because you've learned how to carry it

without breaking.

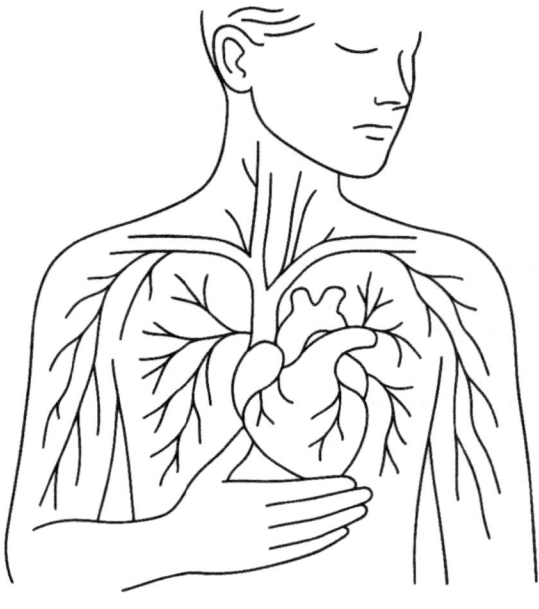

It Wasn't a Mistake

We found each other

in the midst of pain,

naively believing

that love could heal everything.

And what we felt...

was real, was honest,

but we weren't ready.

It wasn't a mistake,

it was an encounter:

an open wound

that revealed what still hurt,

everything we still had to heal.

We saw each other,

but didn't know how to stay.

We felt each other,

but didn't know how to hold on.

And that, too,

is love—

even if it hurts.

Fine Stitching

I'm mending

what others broke in me.

With thread that's soft,

but strong.

With patience,

even when it hurts.

I've learned

not to hide my scars,

but to stitch them

with golden threads

as if they were art.

And you should see...

how beautiful I'm becoming.

Not perfect,

but mine.

Not untouched,

but alive.

Each stitch

brings me back to myself.

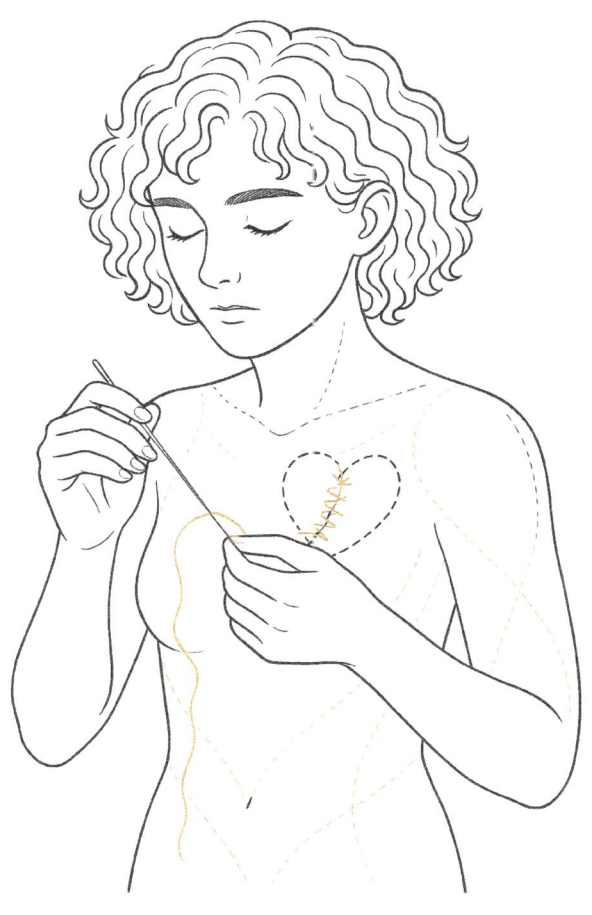

Check Without a Move

Life is like a game of chess—

when you don't understand it,

you're put in checkmate

before you've even made a move.

You arrive at the board with no manual,

no strategy, no allies,

and while you're still blinking,

someone's already taken your rooks,

toppled your queen,

and left you

with a trembling king.

You try to learn the rules

while you're already losing,

while the world shouts:

"Play! Decide! Move!"

and you just stare

at a game you didn't start

but are forced to finish.

Maybe the goal isn't to win,

but to learn to see

the board from above,

to move with calm,

to not fear losing a piece

if your soul can still be saved.

Because even in check,

as long as it's not mate,

you can still hold on.

Sometimes, that too—

is what it means to live.

Selena Santos

What If the Future Doesn't Exist?

And how do you know when the future begins,

if we're always living in the present?

They say time is a line,

but I feel it as a circle,

a heartbeat repeating

between what was

and what never came to be.

We walk with our feet in the now,

staring at shadows of what we once dreamed,

at promises written on calendars

that don't yet exist.

They sell us clocks to measure the waiting,

but no one teaches how to live the moment.

So I ask,

when does the future begin,

if by naming it, it's already the past?

Maybe the future isn't a when,

but a how.

How you choose to see the day that's born,

224

how you decide to love even when it hurts,

how you breathe knowing everything changes.

Because the present is a bridge

and also the shore.

It's the sigh that slips away

before you can ask

if tomorrow has already arrived.

She

She deserves everything

she ever wished for

with every candle she blew out.

Every wish

whispered in silence,

with eyes shut tight

and a heart holding its breath,

hoping the world,

just once,

would listen.

She deserves

the peace she asked for without words,

the hugs she imagined with all her might,

the loves that only lived

inside her tired mind.

Because every year,

in front of the cake and the voices,

she blew with hope

even if no one knew

226

(UN)DONE

how much it hurt to wish

and not receive.

And still,

she kept wishing.

She kept believing

that someday,

some candle,

would give her something more

than just smoke.

What I Want, What I Need

Why can't I have

what I want

when I want it?

Why does life answer me

with silence,

with waiting,

with lessons I never asked for?

And then I get it—

sometimes,

what I want

isn't what I need.

And what I need

doesn't always feel good.

It doesn't always shine.

It doesn't always come when I call.

It's hard to accept

that desire isn't always right,

that urgency doesn't always lead to destiny,

that growing up means

letting go of what you want

to embrace what will heal you.

Even if it hurts.

Even if you don't understand yet.

Even if part of you is still waiting,

you have to accept that sometimes,

what you want

is NOT what you need.

One-Way Ticket

It's a shame

you didn't want to stay.

And it's not arrogance—

but I was the best thing

you were ever going to find—

and you let it go.

You chose the door,

you preferred the silence,

and you hurt me

with the same hands

that once felt like home.

I gave you all my tenderness,

and you traded it

for distance.

You tore the pages

before we even got to write the story.

And the worst part—

you left

as if I never meant a thing to you.

(UN)DONE

You booked your one-way ticket,

without looking back,

without hesitation.

But one day,

when silent nights

start to echo,

you'll remember me—

and you'll know

you held gold in your hands...

and chose to let it go.

How Do You Stop Feeling?

How do you stop feeling

when the heart has no switch,

when everything hurts even in silence,

when even the air reminds you you're alone?

How do you stop loving

someone who didn't stay,

when you would've stayed

a thousand times more?

I don't want to love less,

I just want it to hurt less.

I don't want to go dark,

just rest from the fire.

I've been alone so long

that sometimes I hug myself

with crossed arms,

as if I could convince myself

that it still counts as love.

And yes, I got my hopes up.

And yes, I waited.

(UN)DONE

And yes, I broke again.

But I'm still here.

Feeling.

Because maybe you don't stop feeling.

Maybe you just learn

to let go gently,

to cry without guilt,

to stay with yourself

when no one else will.

THE HEALING

There is no healing here— not the kind we were promised. Because the truth is... you never fully heal. You just learn to live with it. You learn to breathe with the weight inside. You learn to smile even if it still hurts. You learn not to blame yourself for remembering.

What hurts doesn't disappear. It only changes shape. It becomes softer, less urgent. And one day, without realizing it, it stops breaking you.
Acceptance isn't surrender. Acceptance is looking the wound in the eye and saying, "I see you. I'm no longer hiding from you."

Processing it isn't forgetting. It's learning how to carry it without being crushed. It's knowing that even if you can't go back to who you were before, you can still be whole— even if not the same. Like when you break a bone: it heals, but it's never quite the same. It's different. Fragile in changes of weather. Sensitive on gray days. But strong. And yours.

That's what we become after pain: not cured, but rebuilt.

And that's why, every now and then, when nostalgia or memories return, it's not a relapse. It's just the echo of something that existed—and changed you.
It's okay to feel it again. Only this time— you don't let it destroy you.

Healing was never about feeling nothing.
It was about no longer carrying it all.

She Came Back

She came back.

To be honest, I was expecting her.

I had the coffee ready.

We sat and talked.

She made me cry,

reminding me of the past—

that past that still hurts,

those wounds that still bleed

if you touch them too hard.

But she also made me feel strong,

proud

for letting them begin to heal,

for learning to carry them on my skin

without hiding them.

She showed me that, yes,

we've changed,

and what once was

pure darkness

is finally

letting in a bit of light.

She reminded me that I'm still broken,

but now with a few sutures—

and that very soon,

that wound will scar.

And the scar...

will look beautiful on me.

This too will pass

This

is not the end of your story.

It's just a page—

one of those heavy ones,

the kind that hurts to turn,

but doesn't define the whole book.

Right now, it burns.

Right now, it feels like everything.

But it's not.

It's just a dark stretch

on a much longer path,

a pause between chapters,

a knot you'll also learn

how to loosen.

Even if you can't see the "after" today,

even if it feels like everything's falling apart,

believe me:

this too

will pass.

And when you read your whole story,

you'll remember this page

not as the end,

but as the moment

you started moving forward

even with a tired soul.

In the Silence

In the silence of so many nights,

questioning my existence,

I sat with my shadows

and stopped running.

There were no answers.

Only the echo

of all my doubts

bouncing off the walls of my soul.

Why am I here?

Who cares about me?

How long will this weight last?

Why do I feel broken?

But I kept sitting.

I didn't escape.

I didn't pretend to be okay.

I just breathed.

Once.

And then again.

And in the midst of that darkness—

so deeply mine—

I discovered that sometimes

it's not about finding answers,

but learning

to embrace the questions.

Letting them hurt,

but not define me.

Letting them speak,

but not stop me.

Because healing isn't about shining,

it's about placing my hand on my chest again

and feeling that it still beats.

It's saying:

"I'm here,

and for today,

that is enough."

They Tend to Change

And in the end, they're just feelings—

they tend to change.

And for the first time,

I didn't cry.

I didn't beg.

I didn't write poems with your name hidden between

the lines.

I just nodded,

like someone who finally understands

that some things aren't worth hurting over.

Yes, they tend to change,

and mine already did.

They got tired of waiting for you,

of dreaming of you during sleepless dawns.

Now, if I think of you,

it doesn't burn.

If I say your name, I don't shake.

If you leave,

I don't follow you.

Because in the end,

they were just feelings—

and I no longer have the will

to feel for someone

who never stayed.

With Broken Wings

With broken wings,

you keep going.

You move slowly,

closer to the ground,

more aware of the wind against you.

You don't fly high,

but you walk steady.

You don't conquer the sky,

but you learn to love the earth.

Because not everything that breaks

is lost.

And not everything that hurts

stops you.

With broken wings

you learn to move

carefully,

to see differently,

to cherish the simple act

of continuing.

And one day, without warning,

the wounds stop bleeding,

and the wings — though not the same —

lift you again.

Not as high.

But wiser.

More you.

Without Explanation

Some things

have no explanation.

They're simply felt.

Like that sadness that comes without cause,

or that peace that shows up in the midst of chaos.

Like the way someone looks at you

and without saying a word,

puts your soul at ease.

There are pains that can't be understood,

and loves that defy explanation.

There are goodbyes never spoken,

and encounters that logic can't hold.

And that's okay.

Not everything needs a name,

an answer, or a reason.

Sometimes, feeling is the only truth.

And what you don't understand today,

will simply become a part of you

tomorrow.

Still You

You are still you:

brave,

even when you feel broken.

Even if

your hands tremble sometimes,

even if sadness

shows up uninvited,

even if

it hurts to live inside yourself.

You haven't stopped being you.

The one who gets up

with a heart in pieces

and still

walks with dignity.

The one who cries in silence

and blooms in secret.

Because courage

doesn't always shout,

sometimes it just breathes—

and carries on.

And you are still you.

Beautiful,

even with the cracks.

Brave,

even if you don't always see it.

Not Everything Burns Forever

Not everything that begins with fire

is meant to burn forever.

Some flames start out fierce,

but die in silence—

no drama,

no visible ashes,

just the echo of what once was.

Some loves arrive like wildfires,

burning through doubts, fears, shattered corners,

and feel eternal

until the wind shifts

and no longer blows the same.

Sometimes it's not betrayal,

not abandonment,

not blame.

Sometimes it's just time,

wearing down the wood,

quieting the heat

that once felt unstoppable.

Not every love that burns

is meant to last.

And not everything that fades

was a lie.

Sometimes,

love simply leaves.

Not because it wasn't real,

but because it never learned how to stay.

Who Knows

Finally,

I'm learning to enjoy life.

To find beauty in the simple things,

to breathe without rushing,

to laugh without needing permission.

I no longer wait for everything to make sense.

I just let the moment hold me.

And with a little luck,

someday,

I'll share this peace

with the love of my life.

Maybe I'll find them in a book,

or an old song,

or in a gaze that doesn't need words.

Who knows.

For now,

I have myself.

And that, finally,

is starting to be enough.

My Soul

My soul longs for peace—

not because it stopped loving,

but because it has loved too much

without ever finding rest.

It wants to stop begging for affection

in eyes that don't look for it.

It wants to close its eyes

without carrying the ghosts

of what could have been.

It wants to stop fighting to fit

into hearts where it can't fit whole.

Today,

my soul just wants to return to me.

Permission

I'm trying to survive

without losing myself.

Walking slowly

through heavy days

and nights that won't let go.

I no longer want to be the one who always can,

who never falls,

who smiles even while breaking.

Today, I give myself permission

not to be perfect.

To cry without hiding.

To rest without guilt.

To not know where I'm going

but still keep going—

at my own pace.

I'm learning myself again,

without masks,

without goals that aren't mine,

without the obligation to be

what others expected.

Because maybe

being strong isn't about enduring everything...

but knowing when to pause

and stay

—simply—

to listen to your heart.

Last Page

You are still you:

brave,

even when you feel broken.

Because courage

doesn't always roar—

sometimes it trembles.

And even so, you move forward.

With a soul held together by seams,

with memories that no longer weigh the same,

with wounds you've learned

not to hide.

You are still you.

More you than ever.

Not because everything has healed,

but because you chose to stay

with yourself

when everything else seemed to leave.

This isn't the happy ending—

it's the real one.

(UN)DONE

The one chosen without promises.

The one built with what remains

and honored for what lasts.

And you remain.

unbroke,

even if it still aches sometimes.

Free,

even if your voice still shakes.

You are still you.

And that,

that is already enough.

(UN)DONE

Epilogue

*There are things you never forget—
they just learn to hurt in silence.

I've learned not all wounds close the same.
Some stay open,
not to bleed,
but to remind me
of what I survived.

Today, I close this chapter.
Not because I've fully healed,
but because it no longer hurts to remember.

Thank you for what never was.
Thank you for what broke me.
Here ends the unfinished.

And though this story ends here,

The equation remains unsolved.

$\Delta \neq 0$... not yet...

Acknowledgments

To you, Adrian — the love of my life:
Thank you for teaching me what it means to love
without limits. Thank you for the lessons, the
memories, the inspiration. You were, are, and will
always be my muse—the reason so many words found
their shape. I only hope that someday, I can learn to
heal from you.

To my best friend, Nicolas:
Thank you for catching me when I fell and for
celebrating my smallest and greatest victories as if
they were your own. Your presence was a lighthouse
through my longest nights. Thank you.

To my sister, Evelin:
Thank you for your unconditional love, for being that
constant embrace, for being my second mom when I
needed it most. Your support was both root and
refuge along this path.

To Andy:
Thank you for showing up when I needed it. Because
of your convention, I now have two reasons that fill
both my home and my heart—my fur babies, who are
now part of my soul.

And thank you, too,
to those fleeting loves who, without knowing it, added
to my wounds.

And to those soul travelers who, with their brief
presence, contributed threads to my healing.

(UN)DONE

And finally,

 thank you to those reading these pages—
Thank you for opening your heart to words that were
once wounds, sighs, and, eventually, healing.

Selena Santos

Biography

Selena Santos was born in Honduras and currently resides in the United States. She is a Medical Laboratory student who works full-time while nurturing her love for poetry and writing.

Bilingual in Spanish and English, she has found in poetry a way to build bridges between cultures, emotions, and silences.

Driven by solitude and the need to channel emotions that often go unspoken in daily life, she discovered in writing an intimate and liberating refuge.

(UN)DONE is her debut book—a poetic collection that navigates the unspoken, the deeply felt, and the transformed through verse.

Selena writes to heal, to release, and to connect. This is only the beginning of her literary journey, and she plans to continue exploring emotional themes in future works.

(UN)DONE